Index page 64
Crispy chicken p 50
Sweet & Sour Fish 44
Salmon mousse 4

D0536825

CLB 2630
© 1991 Colour Library Books Ltd., Godalming, Surrey, England.
All rights reserved
This edition published 1991 by Gallery Books,
an imprint of W.H Smith Publishers, Inc,
112 Madison Avenue, New York 10016
Colour separations by Hong Kong Graphic Arts Ltd., Hong Kong
Printed and bound in Singapore by Tien Wah Press (PTE) Ltd.,
ISBN 0 8317 5986 0

Gallery Books are available for bulk purchase for sales promotions
and premium use. For details write or telephone
the Manager of Special Sales, WH Smith Publishers, Inc,
112 Madison Avenue, New York, New York 10016 (212) 532-6600

Microwave
Quick `n´ Easy

GALLERY BOOKS

An Imprint of W. H. Smith Publishers Inc.
112 Madison Avenue
New York City 10016

Microwave Quick 'n' Easy

Quick and easy is what microwave cooking is all about. Adapting time-consuming conventional recipes means that you can have all the taste and variety you want in no time at all.

Quick and easy cooking doesn't simply mean opening cans and packets, although you will find recipes here that use convenience foods in creative ways. But there are also many good recipes using fresh ingredients which take an hour or more to cook conventionally, that will cook by microwaves in a fraction of the time. Home-made soups and baked potatoes are good examples of this, as are steamed puddings and meringues.

The list of healthy ingredients used in quick and easy cooking is a long one, and they're all the foods which doctors and dieticians are now telling us we should be eating more of: fresh vegetables, poultry, lean meat, fish and shellfish. The recipes in this chapter introduce many of these foods in simple, delicious dishes with the added convenience of microwave speed.

All microwave recipes were prepared in a 700 watt oven. If your microwave is of a lower output, adjust timings as follows:

500 watt – add 40 seconds for every minute stated in the recipe
600 watt – add 20 seconds for every minute stated in the recipe
650 watt – only a slight increase in the overall time is necessary

QUICK SALMON MOUSSE
SERVES 4

*This very easy recipe makes such an impressive first course, and it
makes a small amount of smoked salmon go a long way.*

1lb salmon
1 bay leaf
4 tbsps water
½ cup low fat soft cheese
½ tsp tomato paste
2 tsps chopped fresh dill
1 tbsp lemon juice
Salt
Dash Tabasco
4 tbsps mayonnaise
4oz sliced smoked salmon
Cucumber slices
Lemon slices
Fresh dill

smooth. Add the reserved liquid as necessary if the
mixture is too thick.

3. Spoon into mounds on 4 small serving dishes
and chill until firm. Before serving, spread 1 tbsp of
mayonnaise carefully over each mound of salmon
mousse.

4. Cut the slices of smoked salmon to size and
press onto the mayonnaise carefully to cover the
mousse completely. Leave at room temperature for
about 30 minutes before serving. Garnish with the
slices of cucumber and lemon and the fresh dill.

Step 3 Spread the
mayonnaise over the
chilled mounds of
fish mousse.

Step 1 Place the fish
in a small casserole
and cover with
pierced plastic wrap
before cooking for
4-6 minutes.

Step 4 Cover the
mayonnaise with
strips of smoked
salmon.

1. Place the fish in a small casserole with the bay
leaf and the water. Cover and cook for 4-6 minutes
on HIGH or until the fish flakes.

2. Remove the skin and bones and put the fish into
a food processor or blender. Reserve the cooking
liquid. Process the fish with the cheese, tomato
paste, lemon juice, dill, salt and Tabasco until

Cook's Notes

TIME: Preparation takes about
15 minutes, and cooking takes
4-6 minutes.

SERVING IDEAS: Serve with
brown bread or toast or melba
toast.

ECONOMY: Trout fillets can be
used instead of salmon.

WATERCRESS SOUP

SERVES 6

Potatoes are used to thicken this pretty green soup. It makes a good dinner party appetizer, hot or cold.

4 medium-sized potatoes, thinly sliced
1 small onion, finely chopped
2 tbsps butter or margarine
3½ cups vegetable or chicken stock
1 bay leaf
Salt and pepper
2 bunches watercress, well washed and thick stems
   removed
½ cup heavy cream
Nutmeg

1. Place the potatoes, onion and butter in a large, deep bowl and cover loosely with plastic wrap or cover partially with a lid. Cook on HIGH for 4-6 minutes or until the potatoes and onions are beginning to soften.

2. Pour on the stock and add the bay leaf, salt and pepper. Re-cover the bowl and cook for a further 8 minutes on HIGH or until the stock just comes to the boil.

3. Allow to cool slightly and pour into a food processor or blender. Reserve 6 small sprigs of watercress for garnish and roughly chop the rest.

4. Place the watercress in the blender or food processor with the soup and purée until smooth. The soup should be lightly flecked with green. Add the cream to the soup, adjust the seasoning and add a pinch of grated nutmeg.

5. Reheat on HIGH for 2-3 minutes before serving. Garnish with the small watercress leaves.

Step 1 Place the potatoes, onion and butter in a large bowl and cover partially to allow the steam to escape.

Step 2 Cook the potatoes in the stock until they soften and the stock has boiled.

Step 4 Purée the potato mixture with the watercress, return to the bowl and stir in the cream by hand.

Cook's Notes

 TIME: Preparation takes about 20 minutes, and cooking takes 14-17 minutes.

 WATCHPOINT: Once the watercress has been added to the soup, reheat only briefly or the soup will lose its color.

 ECONOMY: If desired, omit the cream and replace half the stock with milk.

STILTON AND WALNUT SOUP

SERVES 4

This easy soup tastes as if it took twice as long to make. It makes a delicious appetizer for dinner parties.

3 tbsps butter or margarine
1 large onion, finely chopped
4 tbsps flour
1½ cups chicken stock
1 bay leaf
1 sprig thyme
Salt and pepper
2 cups Stilton cheese, crumbled
1½ cups milk
4 tbsps heavy cream
4 tbsps chopped walnuts

Step 4 Crumble the cheese and stir into the soup with the milk.

Step 6 Sprinkle carefully with the walnuts so that they float on top of the soup.

Step 2 Cook the onion in the butter for about 6 minutes or until very soft.

1. Put the butter or margarine and the onion into a large bowl and cover loosely with plastic wrap, pierced several times.

2. Cook for 6 minutes on HIGH, stirring occasionally. Stir in the flour, add the stock gradually and mix well.

3. Add the bay leaf, thyme and salt and pepper and cook, uncovered, for 10 minutes on HIGH.

4. Remove the herbs and crumble the cheese into the soup. Add the milk and stir to mix well.

5. Cook for 1 minute on HIGH, uncovered.

6. Stir in the cream and cook for a further 1 minute on HIGH. Serve garnished with the chopped walnuts.

Cook's Notes

 TIME: Preparation takes about 10 minutes, and cooking takes about 18 minutes.

 COOK'S TIP: If reheating the soup, start on a MEDIUM setting to prevent the cheese becoming stringy.

 VARIATION: Substitute half Cheddar and half blue cheese for the Stilton if desired. Celery can also be added with the onion for a slightly different flavor.

RED PEPPER SOUP

SERVES 4

Soups are easy both to make and reheat in a microwave oven.
This one has a vibrant color and taste.

3 red peppers
3 tomatoes, seeded and roughly chopped
1 medium onion, finely chopped
4 cups chicken or vegetable stock
Salt and pepper
2 tbsps cornstarch

1. Cut peppers in half and remove seeds. Slice 4 thin strips and reserve. Chop remaining peppers roughly.

2. Place the peppers, tomatoes and onion in a large bowl with the stock, salt and pepper. Stir in the cornstarch. Cover loosely and cook on HIGH for 15 minutes, stirring frequently.

3. Allow the soup to stand for 1-2 minutes and then

Step 1 Cut the peppers in half and remove the cores and seeds completely.

Step 2 Place the vegetables in a large bowl with the stock and stir in the cornstarch.

Step 4 Use the individual microproof bowls for reheating soup. Add the garnish to cook it slightly.

purée in a food processor or blender.

4. Pour the soup into individual microproof bowls and top with reserved pepper strips. Reheat for 1-2 minutes before serving.

Cook's Notes

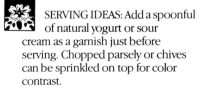

TIME: Preparation takes about 15 minutes, and cooking takes 15 minutes.

SERVING IDEAS: Add a spoonful of natural yogurt or sour cream as a garnish just before serving. Chopped parsely or chives can be sprinkled on top for color contrast.

FREEZING: Allow soup to cool completely and pour into a freezer container. Seal well and freeze for up to 3 months. Defrost on LOW or DEFROST settings for 10 minutes, breaking up the soup as it defrosts. Reheat for 2-3 minutes and add the garnish.

GARLIC VEGETABLES

SERVES 6

Colorful vegetables create a light and different appetizer that can double as a side dish for broiled chicken or fish.

1 small head cauliflower, broken into small flowerets
4oz broccoli
2oz snow peas
½ red pepper, seeded and finely sliced
½ yellow pepper, seeded and finely sliced
4 green onions, thinly sliced on the diagonal
½ cup prepared mayonnaise
2 cloves garlic, crushed
1 tbsp chopped parsley and chives, mixed
Pinch salt and pepper
1 hard-cooked egg, finely chopped, to garnish

Step 2 Add the trimmed snow peas to the broccoli and continue cooking.

Step 2 Cook the broccoli flowerets in a few spoonfuls of water. Stir occasionally to ensure even cooking.

before the end of cooking time.

3. Drain all the vegetables and combine with the sliced red and yellow pepper and the green onions. Mix all the dressing ingredients together and stir carefully into the vegetables. Place the vegetables on serving plates and heat through for 1 minute on HIGH.

4. Garnish with the chopped hard-cooked egg before serving.

Step 3 Toss the vegetables in the dressing, before arranging them on microproof plates.

1. Place the cauliflower flowerets in a casserole with 4 tbsps salted water. Cover and cook on HIGH for 6-8 minutes.

2. Cut the broccoli spears into flowerets the same size as the cauliflower. Place in a casserole with 2 tbsps salted water and cover loosely. Cook on HIGH for 4-5 minutes. Trim the ends of the snow peas and add the pods to the broccoli 1-2 minutes

Cook's Notes

TIME: Preparation takes about 15 minutes, and cooking takes 11-14 minutes. Allow a few minutes standing time for the vegetables before adding them to the peppers and onions.

VARIATION: Other seasonal vegetables may be used in addition to or instead of the ones suggested here.

SERVING IDEAS: Spoon the vegetables onto a bed of lettuce leaves or shredded lettuce. Serve with French bread or melba toast.

CURRIED CHICKEN KEBABS WITH CUCUMBER SAUCE

SERVES 4

As an appetizer or main course, this is a colorful and spicy dish.
Cucumber in yogurt makes a cooling accompaniment.

Step 1 Cut the chicken into strips and combine them with the marinade, coating each piece thoroughly.

Step 2 Thread the marinaded chicken strips onto wooden skewers.

Step 2 Place the kebabs on a microwave roasting rack and cook, turning frequently.

3 chicken breasts, skinned and boned

Marinade
2 tbsps vegetable oil
1 clove garlic, crushed
2 tsps curry powder
¼ tsp cayenne pepper
1 tbsp chopped coriander leaves
Juice and grated rind of 1 lime
Salt and pepper

Sauce
½ cucumber, grated
1 cup plain yogurt
1 tbsp chopped fresh mint
1 tsp mango chutney
Pinch salt and pepper

1. Cut the chicken into 1-inch-wide strips. Combine the ingredients for the marinade and mix with the chicken to coat each piece. Leave to marinate for 1 hour.

2. Thread the chicken onto wooden skewers and place on a microwave roasting rack. Cook for 5 minutes on HIGH, turning the kebabs frequently while cooking.

3. Leave to stand, covered, for 1 minute. While the chicken is marinating, sprinkle the grated cucumber lightly with salt and leave to stand.

4. Rinse thoroughly and pat dry with paper towels. Combine with the remaining sauce ingredients and serve with the chicken kebabs.

Cook's Notes

 TIME: Preparation takes about 10 minutes, plus 1 hour to marinate the chicken. Cooking takes about 5 minutes, plus 1 minute standing time.

 VARIATION: Other herbs and spices may be added to the marinade. Omit the cayenne pepper for a milder flavor.

 ECONOMY: The recipe can be prepared with meat from drumsticks or thighs. Add about 1 minute to the cooking time.

HOT TOMATO SALAD

SERVES 4

This recipe takes only minutes to prepare and cook, yet looks and tastes sensational, either as an appetizer or as a side dish with broiled fish or chicken.

2 large beef tomatoes (total weight about 1¼ lbs)
3 tbsps olive oil
1 tbsp cider vinegar
1 tsp chopped chives
1 tsp roughly chopped basil
½ tsp whole grain mustard

Step 2 Whisk the dressing ingredients together well in a measuring jug for easy pouring.

Step 1 Arrange the tomatoes in a circle in one large or four individual microproof dishes.

Step 3 Check the tomatoes frequently while cooking and baste them occasionally with the dressing.

1. Slice the tomatoes and arrange in a microproof serving dish or in four individual dishes.

2. Mix the oil, vinegar, chives, basil and mustard in a small jug and pour over the tomatoes.

3. Cook, uncovered, on HIGH for 2-3 minutes until

hot but not cooked. If using individual dishes, arrange these in a circle in the microwave. Serve immediately.

Cook's Notes

 TIME: Preparation takes about 5 minutes, and cooking takes 2-3 minutes.

 VARIATION: Basil is the classic herb for tomatoes, but marjoram or dill are good alternatives.

 WATCHPOINT: Tomatoes can quickly overcook and fall apart.

TARRAGON AND LEMON CARROTS

SERVES 4

Tarragon is a lovely alternative to mint with carrots and the flavor of lemon complements them both.

1lb carrots, finely sliced
1 tbsp lemon juice
6 tbsps water
2 sprigs fresh tarragon
Chopped tarragon
Grated lemon zest

1. Put the carrots in a casserole with the lemon juice, water and tarragon.

2. Cover and cook on HIGH for 10-12 minutes.

3. Drain the carrots and discard the tarragon

Step 1 Place the carrots in a casserole with the whole sprigs of tarragon.

sprigs. Garnish with chopped tarragon and lemon zest.

Step 2 Cook, covered with pierced plastic wrap, until the carrots are tender.

Step 3 Sprinkle with lemon zest and chopped tarragon before serving.

Cook's Notes

 TIME: Preparation takes 5 minutes, and cooking takes 10-12 minutes.

 COOK'S TIP: Cooking the stalk as well as the leaves of both tarragon and other herbs will maximize their flavor.

 WATCHPOINT: If carrots overcook in a microwave oven, they will shrivel and toughen.

BAKED POTATOES

SERVES 4

Wrapping potatoes during standing time helps to give them a soft, even texture. Don't be tempted to omit this step.

4 potatoes, 9oz each in weight
½ cup butter mixed with one of the following
  combinations:
1 tbsp chopped chives and 2 tsps Dijon mustard, or
1 tbsp chopped parsley and 2 tsps anchovy paste or
  essence, or
1 tsp chopped basil and 2 tsps tomato paste, or
1 clove garlic, crushed and 1 tbsp crumbled blue
  cheese

Step 1 Prick the potato skins several times with a fork to allow the steam to escape while cooking.

Step 1 Place the potatoes in a circle towards the edge of the turntable. Turn over during cooking.

3. To prepare the butters, place the butter in a small bowl and soften for 20 seconds on HIGH. If the butter is not soft enough to mix, heat for an additional 10 seconds on HIGH.

4. Mix in the chosen flavorings and roll the butter into a cylinder shape in plastic wrap. Chill until firm and then cut into slices to serve.

1. Scrub the potatoes well and pat them dry. Prick them 2 or 3 times with a fork and place in a circle towards the edge of the turntable. Cook for 18 minutes, turning over halfway through cooking.

2. Wrap each potato in foil and allow to stand for 5 minutes before serving. Make a crosswise incision in the top of each potato and press at the sides to open the cuts. Serve with one of the flavored butters.

Step 2 Wrap each potato in foil and leave to stand to finish cooking.

Cook's Notes

 TIME: Preparation takes about 5 minutes, and cooking takes about 18 minutes. Allow 5 minutes standing time to continue cooking the potatoes. Fewer potatoes will take less time to cook.

SERVING IDEAS: Add a green salad or vegetable for a light meal or serve as a side dish with meat, poultry or fish.

$ BUYING GUIDE: Purchase potatoes that are recommended for baking. Red or new potatoes are not good for baking.

VEGETABLE STIR-FRY
SERVES 4

Chinese cooking is fast and so is microwave cooking. Why not combine the two in a crisp and colorful vegetable dish.

2 tbsps oil
4 spears broccoli
4oz miniature corn
4oz snow peas, trimmed
1 red pepper, seeded and sliced
½ cup water chestnuts, sliced
1 cup mushrooms, sliced
1 clove garlic, minced
1 tbsp cornstarch
6 tbsps vegetable stock
4 tbsps soy sauce
2 tbsps sherry
2 cups bean sprouts
2 green onions, sliced

Step 3 Add the other vegetables and toss to coat with the oil.

Step 4 Cook the sauce ingredients until the mixture thickens and clears.

Step 2 Cook the broccoli stalks and the corn in the oil first.

1. Preheat a browning dish according to the manufacturer's directions. Add the oil to the dish when hot.

2. Cut off the broccoli flowerets and reserve them. Slice the stalks diagonally. Slice the miniature sweetcorn in half lengthwise. Put the sliced broccoli stalks and the corn together in the hot oil for 1 minute on HIGH.

3. Add the red pepper, snow peas, water chestnuts, garlic, mushrooms and the broccoli flowerets and cook for a further 1 minute on HIGH.

4. Mix together the cornstarch, vegetable stock, soy sauce and sherry in a glass measure or a small glass bowl and cook for 4 minutes on HIGH, stirring occasionally after 1 minute until thickened.

5. Transfer the vegetables to a serving dish and pour over the sauce. Add the bean sprouts and spring onions and cook for a further 1 minute on HIGH. Serve immediately.

 Cook's Notes

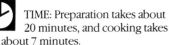 TIME: Preparation takes about 20 minutes, and cooking takes about 7 minutes.

COOK'S TIP: A browning dish may be a slightly expensive piece of microwave equipment, but it is extremely useful for a wide variety of microwave recipes.

 WATCHPOINT: Always follow the manufacturer's directions when using a browning dish as instructions will vary. Be sure to set the dish on a heatproof mat to protect work surfaces.

CONVENIENT VEGETABLE CASSEROLE

SERVES 4

*This is the perfect last minute dish. It can be made with ingredients
you can always keep to hand.*

2 cans mushroom soup or 1 can condensed soup
   with an equal measure of water
2 tbsps cornstarch dissolved in 4 tbsps heavy cream
9-10oz frozen mixed vegetables
Pinch ground nutmeg
1 tbsp chopped parsley
1 packet crisp-fried onions

1. Mix the soup with the cornstarch and heavy cream. Cook, uncovered, on HIGH for 6-7 minutes, stirring occasionally after 1 minute until thickened.

2. Break up the mixed vegetables to separate and add frozen to the sauce. Add the nutmeg and parsley and stir well.

3. Pour into a casserole or serving dish and

Step 2 Break up the frozen vegetables as much as possible before adding them to the sauce.

Step 4 Sprinkle the crisp-fried onions over the surface.

Step 1 Cook the soup and cornstarch together, stirring the mixture occasionally.

microwave on HIGH for 5-8 minutes or until heated through.

4. Sprinkle on the crisp-fried onions and heat for 30 seconds on HIGH. Serve immediately.

Cook's Notes

 TIME: Preparation takes about 5 minutes, and cooking takes about 15 minutes.

 VARIATION: Cream of celery or chicken soup also makes a tasty sauce. Use a single vegetable instead of mixed vegetables, if preferred.

 BUYING GUIDE: Department store food halls and delicatessens are the places to look for crisp-fried onions in jars, packets or vacuum sealed containers.

VEGETABLE PASTA SALAD

SERVES 4

*Pasta cooks to perfection in a microwave oven. There's no chance of
it sticking together and no steam in the kitchen.*

8oz pasta bows
3 cups boiling water
7oz canned tuna
$\frac{2}{3}$ cup corn kernels
$\frac{2}{3}$ cup cooked, sliced green beans
4 green onions, cut diagonally into 1-inch lengths
2 tbsps grated horseradish
1 tbsp lemon juice
4 tbsps mayonnaise
Salt
Freshly ground black pepper
1 tbsp chopped mint
1 tbsp chopped parsley

Step 1 Cover the bowl with plastic wrap, folding one section back to allow steam to escape.

2. Break the tuna into large chunks, add the corn, green beans and onions, and mix together well. Add to the pasta.

3. Mix the horseradish with the lemon juice, mayonnaise and seasoning. Add to the pasta and toss to coat all the salad ingredients. Serve the dish cold, sprinkled with the chopped mint and parsley.

Step 1 Place the pasta in a large bowl and pour on the boiling water.

Step 3 Add the dressing to the pasta and salad ingredients and toss together carefully.

1. Put the pasta into a large bowl with the water. Cover and cook on HIGH for 8-10 minutes until tender. Drain and rinse with cold water, drain again and set aside.

Cook's Notes

TIME: Preparation takes about 5 minutes, and cooking takes 8-10 minutes.

PREPARATION: Most pasta shapes take the same length of time to cook. Exceptions are large shells, lasagne or very fine noodles.

VARIATION: Mint may seem an odd choice for a pasta salad with tuna and horseradish as ingredients, but it tastes very good. Other herbs may be substituted according to your own taste, of course.

SALADE DE LÉGUMES

SERVES 6

This salad is simplicity itself to prepare, yet it is special enough for a dinner party. Follow the latest trend and serve it slightly warm.

9-10oz frozen or canned artichoke hearts
1 red onion, chopped or 4 green onions, thinly sliced
1 clove garlic, minced
1 green pepper, seeded and chopped
1 tsp chopped fresh basil
1 tsp chopped fresh thyme
2 tsps chopped parsley
1lb canned navy beans, white kidney beans or
    butter beans, rinsed and drained
4 tomatoes, peeled, seeded and chopped

Dressing
3 tbsps olive oil
2 tbsps white wine vinegar
½ tsp Dijon mustard
Pinch salt and pepper

1 head Belgian endive and curly endive to garnish

Step 2 Combine all the salad ingredients.

Step 3 Pile the salad onto the prepared salad leaves and spoon over the remaining dressing.

Step 1 Cook frozen artichoke hearts, if using, until warm but not cooked through.

1. If using frozen artichoke hearts, place in a large casserole dish and cover. Microwave on HIGH for

3-4 minutes, or until slightly warm.

2. Stir in the remaining ingredients, except the dressing and garnish, and cook for 2 minutes on HIGH to warm through. Mix together the dressing ingredients, pour over the warm salad and toss to coat.

3. Arrange the Belgian endive and endive leaves on serving plates and pile on the salad. Spoon over any excess dressing to serve. Serve warm.

Cook's Notes

 TIME: Preparation takes about 15 minutes, and cooking takes 2-6 minutes.

 PREPARATION: Mix the dressing into the warm ingredients immediately to help develop their flavors.

 SERVING IDEAS: Serve as a appetizer or as a light main course salad. If desired, add drained, canned tuna.

HAM AND BEAN FRIED RICE

SERVES 4

This makes an interesting side dish for a complete Chinese meal or a light main course on its own. Ham and the egg strips give it more substance.

3 tbsps oil
2 eggs, beaten
½ cup ham, chopped
1 cup rice, cooked
4oz green beans, cut in thin, diagonal slices
1 tbsp soy sauce
4 green onions, chopped

Step 1 Pour the egg mixture onto the hot surface of the browning dish.

Step 2 Turn the egg pancakes over to cook the second side.

1. Heat a browning dish for 5 minutes on HIGH. Pour in half the oil and half the beaten egg and cook for 30 seconds on HIGH on one side.

2. Turn over and cook for 30 seconds on the second side. Repeat with the remaining egg. Keep the egg warm.

3. Add the remaining oil to the dish. Heat for 1 minute on HIGH and add the ham. Cover the dish and cook for 1 minute on HIGH. Add the rice and

cook, covered, for 5 minutes on HIGH. Add the beans, soy sauce and onions. Cook for 1 minute on HIGH and toss the ingredients to mix well.

4. Slice the eggs into thin strips and scatter over the top of the rice. Cover the dish and leave to stand for 2 minutes before serving.

Step 3 Cook the rice and other ingredients until the vegetables are tender but still crisp.

Cook's Notes

 TIME: Preparation takes about 15 minutes, and cooking takes about 9 minutes, plus 2 minutes standing time.

PREPARATION: Once the egg strips have been cooked, they can be kept warm but will toughen if reheated.

$ BUYING GUIDE: There are several different types of browning dishes available. If yours does not have a lid, the ingredients in step 3 can be cooked in any type of microproof covered dish.

ASPARAGUS AND TOMATO OMELET

SERVES 2

_A microwave oven can help you cut calories. Even omelets cook
without butter and without sticking._

4oz chopped asparagus, fresh or frozen
2 tbsps water
4 eggs, separated
6 tbsps milk
1 tsp flour
Salt and pepper
2 tomatoes, peeled, seeded and chopped
3 tbsps grated cheese
Paprika

the dish and cook on MEDIUM for 7 minutes or
until softly set.

4. Lift the edges of the omelet as it cooks to allow
the uncooked mixture to spread evenly.

5. Sprinkle with the cheese and spread on the
drained asparagus and the chopped tomato. Fold
over and cook for 1 minute on LOW to melt the
cheese. Sprinkle with paprika and serve immediately.

Step 2 Beat the egg
whites until stiff peaks
form then fold them
into the egg yolk
mixture.

Step 3 Pour the
omelet mixture into
the pie dish.

1. Put the asparagus and water into a large
casserole. Cover and cook for 5-6 minutes on
HIGH. Leave to stand while preparing the omelet.

2. Beat the egg yolks, milk, flour and salt and
pepper together. Beat the egg whites until stiff but
not dry and fold into the egg yolks.

3. Melt the butter in a 9 inch glass pie pan for
30 seconds on HIGH. Pour the omelet mixture into

Step 4 Lift the edges
of the omelet as it
cooks to allow the
mixture to spread and
cook evenly.

Cook's Notes

 TIME: Preparation takes about
15 minutes, and cooking takes
about 15 minutes.

 VARIATION: Use your
imagination to create new filling
ideas with different cheeses,
vegetables or seafood.

 COOK'S TIP: Using the MEDIUM
or 50% setting will ensure a
light, fluffy omelet that doesn't
toughen during cooking or on
standing.

SWISS CHEESE LAYER

SERVES 4

_The nutty taste of Emmental and the creamy taxture of Gruyère turn
simple baked eggs into something special._

1 cup grated Emmental cheese
1 tbsp chopped borage
4 eggs
Salt and pepper
1 cup grated Gruyère cheese
2 tsps savory
¼ cup corn chips, broken

1. Mix the Emmental cheese and borage together
and divide between 4 custard cups.

2. Crack 1 egg into each dish and season to taste
with salt and pepper. Prick egg yolks once with a
knife.

3. Mix the Gruyère cheese with the savory and use
to top each dish.

4. Sprinkle with the broken corn chips, arrange in
a circle and cook on LOW for 3-5 minutes until the
cheese melts and the eggs are cooked.

Step 1 Mix the cheese
and borage together
and divide between
four custard cups or
individual microproof
dishes.

Step 2 Prick the egg
yolks once with a
sharp knife to prevent
them bursting.

Cook's Notes

TIME: Preparation takes about
5 minutes, and cooking takes
3-5 minutes.

VARIATION: Try other types of
cheese and herbs for different
flavor combinations.

PREPARATION: When cooking
with cheese in a microwave
oven, use a LOW or MEDIUM setting
to avoid toughening the cheese.

SCRAMBLED EGGS AND SHRIMP

SERVES 4

*A microwave oven makes easy work of scrambling eggs. They turn
out much lighter and fluffier than when conventionally cooked.*

4 tsps butter or margarine
4 eggs
4 tbsps milk or light cream
1 tbsp chopped chives
1/3 cup cooked, peeled shrimp
4 large ripe tomatoes
Salt and pepper

Step 3 Stir the eggs frequently while cooking so they cook evenly.

1. Place the butter in a glass measure or a small, deep bowl and cook on HIGH for 30 seconds-1 minute.

2. Beat the eggs with the milk or cream and add a pinch of salt and pepper. Pour into the melted butter and cook on HIGH for 3-4½ minutes.

3. Stir frequently while cooking to bring the set pieces of egg from the outside of the bowl to the center.

4. When just beginning to set, remove the eggs

from the oven and stir in the chives and the shrimp. Allow to stand for 1-2 minutes to finish cooking.

5. Meanwhile, cut the tomatoes into quarters or eighths but do not cut all the way through the base. Arrange the tomatoes in a circle on the turntable and heat through for 1-2 minutes on HIGH.

6. To serve, press the tomatoes open slightly and fill each with some of the egg and shrimp mixture.

Step 4 When just beginning to set, stir in the chives and the shrimp. Cover completely before leaving to stand.

Step 6 Fill the cut tomatoes with the egg mixture.

Cook's Notes

 TIME: Preparation takes about 15 minutes, and cooking takes 5-7 minutes plus 1-2 minutes standing time.

 VARIATION: Diced ham may be substituted for the shrimp or for a vegetarian dish, use about 2oz chopped mushrooms.

 WATCHPOINT: The cooking time for the tomatoes will vary according to their ripeness.

OEUFS EN COCOTTE

SERVES 4

This is an easy appetizer, but very tasty and relatively inexpensive.
It also makes a quick and delicious lunch

1 tbsp butter or margarine
4oz mushrooms, chopped
2 tbsps flour
4 tbsps dry white wine
2 tbsps milk
2 tsps chopped mixed herbs
1 tbsp capers, chopped
Salt and pepper
4 eggs
4 tbsps heavy cream
Paprika
Nutmeg

1. Place the butter in a small casserole and melt on HIGH for 30 seconds. Add the chopped mushrooms and cook for 2 minutes on HIGH.

2. Stir in the flour and add the wine and milk. Cook for a further 1-2 minutes on HIGH, or until thickened. Add the capers, mixed herbs and salt and pepper to taste.

Step 2 Cook the sauce ingredients in a small casserole until very thick.

3. Divide the mixture into 4 custard cups and make a well in the center of the mixture in each dish.

Step 3 Spoon the sauce mixture into custard cups and make a well in the center to hold the eggs.

4. Break an egg into the center of the mixture in each cup. Pierce the yolk once with a sharp knife. Cook for 3-4 minutes on HIGH or until the white is set and the yolk is still soft.

5. Place a spoonful of cream on top of each egg and sprinkle with paprika and grated nutmeg. Cook for 1 minute on LOW to heat the cream. Serve immediately.

Step 5 When the eggs are cooked, spoon on the cream and sprinkle with paprika and nutmeg.

Cook's Notes

 TIME: Preparation takes about 10 minutes, and cooking takes about 9 minutes.

 VARIATION: Use chopped green or black olives in place of the capers. Chopped ham makes a tasty addition.

 PREPARATION: Piercing the egg yolk will prevent it bursting by allowing steam to escape.

VEAL AND GARLIC CHEESE ROLLS

SERVES 4

*Tender veal needs quick cooking and a microwave oven fulfils that
while keeping all the natural juices in the meat.*

4-6oz veal escalopes
2 small cloves garlic, crushed
8oz low fat, soft cheese
Small bunch chives, chopped
Salt
Freshly ground black pepper
1 tsp paprika (optional)

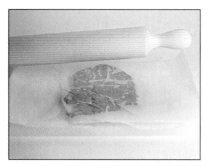

Step 1 Place each escalope between sheets of wax paper and flatten, using a rolling pin.

1. Flatten the veal escalopes between 2 sheets of wax paper using a rolling pin and taking care to keep each escalope in one piece. Set aside.

2. Combine the garlic, cheese and chives together and season with salt and pepper.

3. Spread a quarter of the mixture over each of the veal escalopes and roll up like a jelly roll. Sprinkle

with paprika if desired.

4. Arrange in a circle in a dish and cook, uncovered, on HIGH for 8-10 minutes. Serve immediately.

Step 3 Spread each escalope with some of the cheese mixture, roll up and sprinkle with paprika.

Step 4 Arrange the rolls in the dish, either all together in a circle or, if large, two at a time side by side.

Cook's Notes

 TIME: Preparation takes about 10 minutes, and cooking takes 8-10 minutes.

 SERVING IDEAS: Buttered pasta and a green salad make good accompaniments.

COOK'S TIP: Paprika sprinkled onto savory food before microwaving gives it a good brown color and makes it look more appetizing.

TROUT WITH ALMONDS

SERVES 4

Whole fish cook beautifully in a microwave oven and there is less chance of the fish falling apart. They stay moist and flavorful, too.

½ cup butter
½ cup flaked almonds
4 even-sized trout, cleaned
Watercress
Lime slices or wedges

1. Preheat a browning dish according to the manufacturer's instructions. Add half the butter and heat until beginning to brown.

2. Add the almonds and stir to brown slightly. Remove the almonds and the browned butter to a dish and set aside.

3. Pat the trout dry. Reheat the browning dish. Melt the remaining butter and, when very hot, add two of the trout and cook on HIGH for 2 minutes.

4. Turn the trout over and cook for a further 2 minutes. Reposition the trout occasionally during cooking. Repeat with the remaining two trout.

5. Serve the trout topped with the almonds and any remaining butter. Garnish with watercress and lime.

Step 2 Add the almonds and cook to brown lightly, stirring constantly. If the dish is sufficiently hot, do this outside the oven.

Step 1 In a preheated browning dish, heat the butter until beginning to brown.

Step 4 When the trout have browned on one side, turn them over and cook the other side.

Cook's Notes

 TIME: Preparation takes about 10 minutes, and cooking takes about 4 minutes per fish.

 VARIATION: Use other types of nuts or substitute herbs and simply cook them for 30 seconds in melted butter.

 SERVING IDEAS: Accompany the trout with new potatoes and asparagus for an early summer meal or with rice and a seasonal vegetable.

SWEET AND SOUR FISH

SERVES 4

Fish fillets cook much better in a microwave oven than they do by conventional methods. This sauce adds zip to mild whitefish.

1lb sole or plaice fillets
4oz canned, sliced water chestnuts
8oz canned pineapple chunks, ½ cup juice reserved
1 green pepper, seeded and sliced
Juice of 1 lemon
1-2 tbsps brown sugar
1 tbsp light soy sauce
1 tbsp tomato ketchup
1 tbsp cornstarch
3 green onions, shredded
3 tomatoes, peeled and quartered
Salt and pepper

1. Skin the fish fillets and fold them in half. Place them in a large casserole, with the thinner ends of the fillets towards the middle of the dish. Pour over enough water to come ½-inch up the sides of the fillets. Cover the dish loosely and cook for 2 minutes on HIGH.

2. Set aside and keep warm. Drain the water chestnuts and place them in a small bowl with the pineapple chunks and the green pepper.

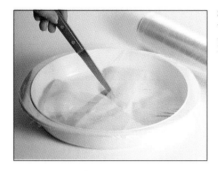

Step 1 Cover the dish with plastic wrap, piercing it several times with a sharp knife.

3. Mix the reserved juice from the pineapple with the lemon juice, brown sugar, soy sauce, ketchup, and cornstarch. Pour this over the pineapple, water chestnuts and green pepper in a small bowl and cook for 2-3 minutes on HIGH, stirring often until thickened.

4. Drain off the cooking liquid from the fish. Add the tomatoes, green onions, salt and pepper to the sauce. Cook for a further 1 minute on HIGH.

5. Arrange the fish on a serving plate and pour over the sauce.

Step 1 Place the fish fillets in a shallow casserole, thin ends to the center.

Step 2 The fish should still feel slightly firm to the touch when cooked. Cover completely and set aside to finish cooking.

Cook's Notes

 TIME: Preparation takes about 15 minutes, and cooking takes 4-5 minutes.

 SERVING IDEAS: Rice or Oriental noodles are delicious with this dish.

 COOK'S TIP: Cornstarch sauces actually cook better in a microwave oven than they do on top of the stove. Allow to cook for 1 minute before stirring.

STUFFED BACON CHOPS
SERVES 4

A stuffing of rice and prunes flavored with fresh sage makes bacon interesting enough for dinner guests.

4 thick bacon chops
1 tbsp oil
1 small onion, peeled and finely chopped
1oz macadamia nuts, chopped
¾ cup cooked rice
¼ cup dried prunes, stoned and chopped
1 tbsp chopped sage
Freshly ground black pepper
Salt
2 tbsps butter

1. Carefully cut a slit down the side of each bacon chop. Put the oil, onion and nuts into a small bowl and cook, uncovered, on HIGH for 2 minutes.

Step 1 Cut a slit in the side of each chop to form a pocket for the stuffing.

2. Stir in the rice, prunes, sage, salt and pepper. Cover and cook on HIGH for 2-4 minutes until hot. Pack the stuffing into each chop.

Step 2 Spoon some stuffing into each pocket, spreading it out evenly.

3. Heat a browning dish according to the manufacturer's instructions. Add the butter and quickly add the chops, press down slightly and turn browned side up.

Step 3 Place the chops in the preheated browning dish and press them down to seal and brown.

4. Cook, uncovered, on HIGH for 4 minutes or until cooked through.

Cook's Notes

 TIME: Preparation takes about 10 minutes, and cooking takes 8-9 minutes.

 VARIATION: Macadamia nuts are expensive, but other nuts such as almonds may be used instead.

 SERVING IDEAS: With rice in the stuffing, these chops need only a salad or green vegetables.

HERB LAMB NOISETTES

SERVES 4

*A browning dish is what gives these succulent pieces of boned lamb
their appetizing color with no messy broiler pan.*

1 large onion, peeled and chopped
1 tbsp oil
7oz canned chopped tomatoes
1 small clove garlic, peeled and crushed
1 tsp marjoram
1 tsp oregano
1 cup button mushrooms
4oz noisettes of lamb
Knob butter

place the noisettes in the dish and press each one
down firmly, then turn them over and press down
again. Cook on HIGH for 5 minutes.

4. Transfer the noisettes to a warm serving dish
and, if necessary, reheat the sauce for 1 minute on
HIGH. Remove string from noisettes. Serve the
sauce poured over the noisettes.

Step 1 Cook the onion in the oil until soft and translucent.

Step 2 Combine with all the other sauce ingredients and cook until bubbling and thickened.

Step 3 Press the noisettes against the surface of the browning dish to color the meat and fat lightly.

1. Put the onion and oil in a small bowl and cook
on HIGH for 3 minutes, until soft.

2. Add the tomatoes, garlic, herbs and mushrooms.
Cook, uncovered, on HIGH for 3 minutes, stirring
once. Set aside and keep warm.

3. Heat a large browning dish for the manufacturer's
recommended time. Add the butter and quickly

Cook's Notes

 TIME: Preparation takes
10 minutes, and cooking takes
11 minutes.

VARIATION: Use your favorite
choice of herbs – basil and
rosemary are also delicious with
lamb.

 SERVING IDEAS: Serve with
potatoes and a green vegetable,
or serve rice or pasta to go with the
sauce.

 BUYING GUIDE: The butcher
will bone a best end neck of
lamb for you and tie and cut
noisettes. If doing this yourself, do
not tie the strings too tightly.

CRISPY CHICKEN

SERVES 4-6

Chicken cooks so well in a microwave oven, and a crisp topping gives both visual and taste appeal.

3½lbs chicken pieces
1 cup crushed cornflakes
6 tbsps grated Parmesan cheese
½ tsp mustard powder
1 tsp paprika
½ tsp celery salt
½ tsp oregano
½ tsp parsley
Pepper
½ cup butter or margarine
2 eggs, beaten

1. Skin all the chicken pieces and remove any fat. Combine the cornflakes, cheese, herbs, spices and pepper and spread out evenly on a sheet of wax paper.

2. Melt the butter for 1 minute on HIGH and stir into the beaten eggs in a shallow dish. Dip the chicken into the egg and butter mixture or use a basting brush to coat each piece.

Step 2 Dip the chicken in the butter and egg mixture, or use a pastry brush to coat them with it.

3. Put the chicken pieces in the crumb mixture and lift the ends of the paper to help toss the chicken, coating each piece evenly.

Step 3 Place the chicken in the cornflake mixture, coating both sides evenly.

Step 5 Rearrange the chicken pieces halfway through cooking, keeping the thickest parts to the outside of the dish.

4. Place half the chicken in a glass dish, bone side down. Make sure the thickest pieces of the chicken are on the outside of the dish to start. Cover them loosely with wax paper. Cook on HIGH for 9-12 minutes.

5. Rearrange and turn the chicken over halfway through the cooking time, and remove the paper. Keep the cooked chicken warm while cooking the remaining chicken.

6. If necessary, cover the turntable with paper towels to reheat all of the chicken at once for 1-2 minutes.

Cook's Notes

 TIME: Preparation takes 15 minutes, and cooking takes 9-12 minutes. Allow 1-2 minutes to reheat the chicken, if necessary.

 COOK'S TIP: Keep the thickest part of the food to the outside to ensure even cooking.

 SERVING IDEAS: Serve hot with one of the vegetable dishes or refrigerate and serve cold. Good for picnics and buffets.

PLUMS IN PORT

SERVES 4

This quick dessert can be cooked at the last minute with the minimum of preparation. That's the beauty of cooking with microwaves.

3 cups granulated sugar
1½ cups ruby port or red wine
2 whole cloves or 1 cinnamon stick
1½lbs plums, halved and pitted

1. Put the sugar and port or wine into a large, deep bowl. Put in the cloves or cinnamon stick and cook, uncovered, for 4-8 minutes on HIGH, stirring occasionally to help dissolve the sugar.

Step 2 Add the plums to the liquid and partially cover the bowl.

Step 1 Combine the sugar, port and whole spices in a large, deep bowl. Cook uncovered, stirring occasionally.

3. Reduce the power to MEDIUM and cook for a further 5 minutes. Uncover and allow plums to cool slightly.

Step 3 Test the plums with a knife. They should just be starting to soften when removed from the microwave.

2. Add the plums to the syrup, cover the bowl with plastic wrap and cook for 5 minutes on HIGH.

Cook's Notes

 TIME: Preparation takes about 10 minutes, and cooking takes about 14 minutes.

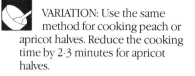 VARIATION: Use the same method for cooking peach or apricot halves. Reduce the cooking time by 2-3 minutes for apricot halves.

 SERVING IDEAS: Serve either warm or cold with whipped cream or ice cream.

STEAMED RASPBERRY JAM PUDDING

SERVES 6

Steamed puddings can take hours to cook on top of the stove. Turn to your microwave oven for a traditional treat to suit modern schedules.

½ cup raspberry jam
½ cup butter or margarine
½ cup sugar
2 eggs
1 tsp vanilla extract
1 cup all-purpose flour
1 tsp baking powder
2 tbsps milk

1. Grease a 3 cup mixing bowl or decorative mold thoroughly with butter or margarine. Put the jam into the bottom of the mold and set aside.

Step 1 Spoon the raspberry jam into the bottom of a well-buttered bowl or mold.

2. Cream the remaining butter or margarine with the sugar until light and fluffy.

3. Beat in the eggs one at a time and add the vanilla extract. Sift in the flour and baking powder and then fold in. If the mixture is too stiff, add up to

2 tbsps of milk to make a soft dropping consistency.

4. Spoon the mixture carefully on top of the jam and smooth the top. Cover the bowl or mold with 2 layers of plastic wrap, pierced several times to release the steam.

5. Cook for 5-8 minutes on HIGH. Leave to stand for 5-10 minutes before turning out to serve.

Step 3 Add milk if necessary to make the batter of a dropping consistency.

Step 5 When the pudding is done, it will still look slightly damp on top but will firm up on standing.

Cook's Notes

 TIME: Preparation takes 15-20 minutes, and cooking takes 5-8 minutes plus 5-10 minutes standing time.

 VARIATION: Use other flavors of jam, preserves or marmalades. Golden raisins, dates or chopped nuts can be added to the batter before cooking.

SERVING IDEAS: Serve warm with whipped or pouring cream, ice cream or custard sauce.

CHOCOLATE MOUSSE

SERVES 4

This luxurious pudding with a French accent is always a favorite for dinner parties, but when it's this easy to make, why restrict it to special occasions?

7 tbsps unsalted butter
4 tbsps sugar
4 eggs, separated
8oz semi-sweet chocolate
4 tbsps coffee liqueur
Whipped cream and coffee dragées or grated chocolate to garnish

and fluffy.

4. Whip the egg whites and fold into the mixture. Spoon into small dessert dishes and chill until firm. Decorate with a rosette of whipped cream and one coffee dragée or sprinkle with grated chocolate. Serve cold.

Step 1 Heat the butter until very soft, but not melted.

Step 2 Use a medium setting to melt the chocolate with the liqueur until smooth.

Step 3 Beat the chocolate into the butter and egg mixture until very light and fluffy.

1. Put the butter into a deep bowl and soften for 30 seconds on HIGH. Add the sugar and beat until light and fluffy. Gradually beat in the egg yolks.

2. Chop the chocolate roughly and place in a small bowl with the coffee liqueur. Microwave on MEDIUM for 2 minutes or until the chocolate has completely melted.

3. Combine the chocolate with the butter mixture and beat for 5 minutes or until the mixture is light

Cook's Notes

 TIME: Preparation takes about 15 minutes, and cooking takes about 2-3 minutes plus several hours chilling time.

 VARIATION: Different liqueurs can be used to suit your own taste. You can substitute brandy, orange or raspberry liqueurs or crème de menthe.

 PREPARATION: The mousse can be prepared in advance and refrigerated overnight without any change in the consistency.

MICROWAVE MERINGUES

SERVES 8-10

These are as much fun to make as they are delicious to eat. They grow magically before your eyes.

1 egg white
1lb powdered sugar (all the sugar may not be needed)
Food colorings such as red, green or yellow
Chopped toasted nuts or sifted cocoa powder
Flavoring extract
Powdered sugar
Whipped cream

1. Beat the egg white lightly and sift in the powdered sugar until the mixture forms a pliable paste that can be rolled out like pastry. Add the chosen coloring and flavoring with the powdered sugar. The mixture may also be divided and several different colorings and flavoring used.

Step 1 Mix the egg white with enough sifted powdered sugar to make a pliable dough.

2. Roll the dough to a thin sausage shape about ½ inch thick. Cut into small pieces and place well apart on wax paper on a plate or microwave cookie sheet. Flatten the pieces slightly.

3. Cook for 1 minute on HIGH or until dry. The meringues will triple in size. Leave to cool on a wire rack.

4. When the meringues are cool, sandwich them together with whipped cream and sprinkle lightly with powdered sugar.

Step 2 Roll the dough into a thin sausage shape.

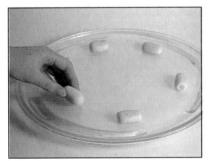

Step 2 Cut each sausage into small pieces and arrange them in a circle, leaving ample space for the meringues to triple in size. Do this in batches, if necessary.

Cook's Notes

TIME: Preparation takes about 15 minutes, and cooking takes about 6 minutes.

VARIATION: The meringue mixture may be rolled to a ½-inch thickness and a very small pastry cutter used to cut out different shapes. These meringues will be slightly larger than those made by the first method.

SERVING IDEAS: Serve with a fresh fruit salad, fruit or chocolate sauce, if desired.

CHOCOLATE RING CAKE

SERVES 6-8

_Cakes bake in about a quarter of the time they take in a
conventional oven. This one has an easy topping, too._

1½ cups all-purpose flour
1½ tsps bicarbonate of soda
4 tbsps cocoa
1 cup sugar
¾ cup evaporated milk
1 tbsp white vinegar
⅔ cup butter or margarine
2 eggs, beaten
Few drops vanilla extract
4oz white chocolate

1. Lightly grease a 6 cup cake ring. Sift the flour,
soda and cocoa into a mixing bowl and add the
sugar. Combine the evaporated milk and vinegar
and set aside.

2. Melt the butter or margarine on HIGH for
2-3 minutes or until liquid. Pour into the milk and
vinegar and gradually add the beaten eggs. Stir in
the vanilla extract. Pour into the cake ring and
smooth down the top to level.

Step 2 Pour the liquid
ingredients into the
dry ones and mix
together quickly. The
vinegar and soda will
bubble.

3. Cook on HIGH for 10 minutes or until top of the
cake is only slightly sticky. Cool in the ring for
10 minutes then turn out onto a wire rack to cool
completely.

Step 3 When the
cake is done, the top
will still be slightly
sticky to the touch.

4. Melt the white chocolate in a small dish for
1-2 minutes on HIGH or until liquid. When the cake
is cool, drizzle over the still warm white chocolate
and allow to set completely before cutting the cake
to serve.

Step 4 When the
cake has cooled
completely, drizzle
with melted white
chocolate to make a
lacy pattern.

Cook's Notes

 TIME: Preparation takes about
20 minutes, and cooking takes
about 10 minutes, plus 10 minutes
standing time.

 VARIATION: For a completely
dark chocolate cake decorate
with the same amount of semi-sweet
chocolate or use milk chocolate.

FREEZING: Plain cake can be
frozen for up to 2 months.
Defrost at room temperature or use
the DEFROST setting for 2 minutes
then set aside at room temperature
to finish defrosting. Decorate with
chocolate once the cake has
defrosted.

FIG AND APRICOT CHARLOTTES

SERVES 6

Try this deceptively easy pudding for your next dinner party. It looks impressive and as if it took hours to make!

1¼ cups dried figs
1¼ cups dried apricots
½ cup brandy
1lb cream or curd cheese
½ cup thick natural yogurt
3 tbsps honey
Halved toasted almonds
½ cup heavy cream
Nutmeg

1. Place the figs and the apricots in a deep bowl with the brandy and heat for 30 seconds-1 minute on HIGH. Leave to stand, covered, for 2-3 minutes. Drain off the brandy and reserve.

2. Place a circle of wax paper in the bottom of 6 custard cups. Cut the figs in half and press them flat. Press the apricots to flatten slightly. Use the fruit to line the sides of the dishes, with the seed side of the fig to the inside.

3. Soften the cream or curd cheese for 30 seconds-1 minute on MEDIUM. Stir in the yogurt, honey and the reserved brandy.

4. Spoon the mixture into the custard cups, pressing it down firmly against the base and the fruit lining the sides. Fold any fruit ends over the cheese filling and chill.

5. Turn the charlottes out onto a serving plate and pour cream carefully around the base of each. Remove the paper circles from the top and decorate with toasted almonds and freshly grated nutmeg.

Step 1 Heat the figs and apricots in the brandy to flavor and soften them.

Step 2 Cut the figs and apricots to fit the dishes and use alternately to line the sides.

Step 4 Fill the dishes with the softened cheese mixture, pressing it in well.

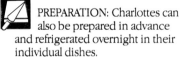 _Cook's Notes_

TIME: Preparation takes about 20 minutes, and cooking takes 1-2 minutes.

PREPARATION: Charlottes can also be prepared in advance and refrigerated overnight in their individual dishes.

FREEZING: Wrap well and freeze in the individual dishes for up to 1 month. Defrost overnight in the refrigerator and then leave at room temperature for 1 hour before serving.

Edited by Jane Adams and Jillian Stewart
Photographed by Peter Barry
Recipes Prepared and Styled for Photography by Bridgeen Deery
and Wendy Devenish
Designed by Claire Leighton, Sally Strugnell and Alison Jewell